HER-ME
And the Tree

written by

Josie C. Daniels
(Little Jo)

First published by Busybird Publishing 2017
Copyright © 2017 Josie Daniels

ISBN 978-1-925585-91-9

This book is copyright. Apart from any fair dealing for the purposes of study, research, criticism, review, or as otherwise permitted under the Copyright Act, no part may be reproduced by any process without written permission. Enquiries should be made through the publisher.

This is a work of fiction. Any similarities between places and characters are a coincidence.

Cover design: Busybird Publishing
Layout and typesetting: Busybird Publishing

Busybird Publishing
2/118 Para Road
Montmorency Victoria
Australia 3094
www.busybird.com.au

DEDICATED TO HER-ME

Her-me (meaning her and me)

Gone but not forgotten, you were there when no one was, you came to talk to me when no one did.

The joy you gave me, when you were here, my little friend, how I miss you, that's clear.

Thank you for being my lovely pet, you are missed and loved with all my might, you loved your baths, and going to the park, and we sat together side by side, you watched me draw and watch the telly, you loved the car, and we travelled far, you loved the birds, when we sat outside, and they come to see you still today, how we miss you everyday, why did you have to go this way.

I wish you were here today, with love my little friend, thank you for the joy you gave me, never be forgotten, I take you in my heart, may we never be apart.

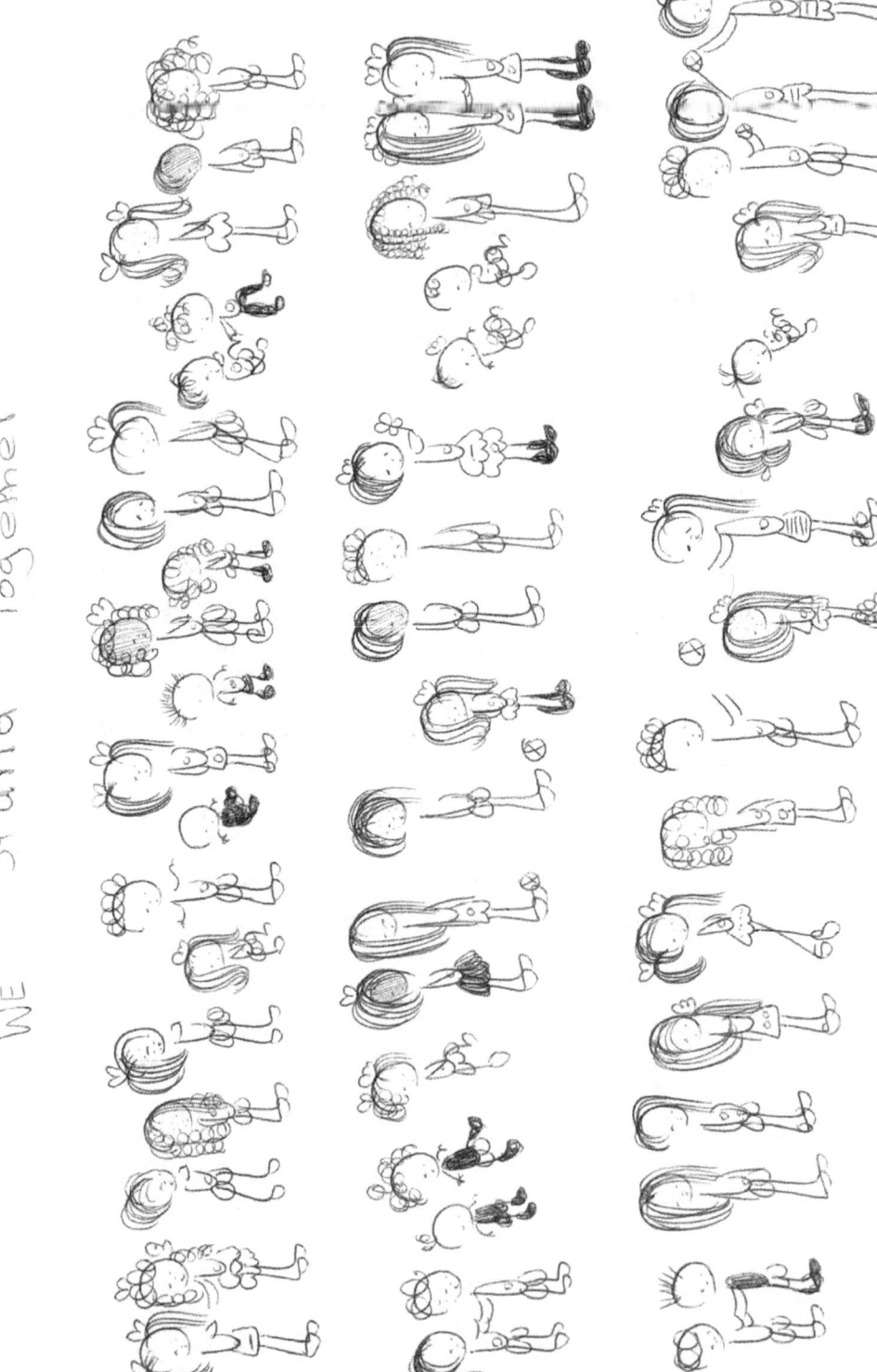

We Stand Together

Dedication

Blaise + staff, Christina and Rob, my mum + dad + family, Davi + Leah, Malcolm, Elisa, Owen, Heath, Steve F, Ivan D, Eva, Ray, Mandy + Family, Karl, Roger, Hellena + Toni, Henny, Rei, Keith, Frank, Colin, Tilik, Grace, Rob + Sean, Brendan. To those who work hard to provide us amazing food. Thank you for the great food and your hard work, Irma.

To those who have supported me in my tough times,

I thank you,

To those I haven't mentioned I thank you,

To those that have read my book, I thank you –

    To all pets.

Contents

With Thoughts and Thanks	2
Jo's Special Willow Tree	4
Fun to Be	5
Dedication	6
The Open Door	7
Future to Be	8
Walking to the Future	9
Deep Words	10
Hope	11
Expressions	12
To Fly Away	13
A Reflection on One Self	14
Bonded	15
Inspired	16
The Sand Through Our Eyes	17
Lost and Gone	18
The Friend in You	19
Friends	20
The Waterfall	21
Brothers and Sisters	23

Our World	24
To Remember	25
Closely Near	26
Shining Star	27
Because of You	28
A Pet's Friend	29
Clouds of Wonder	30
Never Easy	31
Mum	32
Not to be Forgotten	33
Always a Person	34
Nature	35
My Journey so Far	36
To Belong	37

With Thoughts and Thanks

To my dear friend Malcolm, for helping me,
for without your support I would be lost.

To my dear friend Elisa, what a lovely dear
friend you are.

To dear Ivan D, for all your running around
for me, being beside me when I was not well.
You are a good friend.

To Owen, for laughing at all my jokes,
for being a good friend, I thank you.

To Heath, for our laughs, we have fun
for this I thank you my friend.

To Davi every day you take the
time for me, always finding the time for me,
our friendship strong, my lovely friend, so dear
you are.

To Roger, thank you for listening to me when I
needed a shoulder, for your patience, for your
understanding, my friend I thank you.

To Henny, for making me laugh, I thank you.
Also a lovely person full of character.

To Blaise + staff.
Thank you for making
my dream come true.

To Christina, Her-me brought us together, my friend, thank you for being there,
thank you for your support.

To Hellena, for reconnecting our friendship.
Thank you for making me laugh my friend.

To those that have passed on may you not
be forgotten, with thoughts of all of you.

To my mum and dad and family.

To all who read my poems, I hope I inspire.
I thank you.

To God, I thank you for giving me these
wonderful people to take this journey with
me.

To those who have touched my life I thank you.

Jo's Special Willow Tree

Picture a cool breeze on a mountain.
Raindrops slowly dripping,
one willow tree swaying from side,
to side, with shades a lovely green
colour, which hang in a beautiful way.

Picture a lonely young boy under this
tree, raindrops forming the tears as he
fell to his knees, looking up at the tree
(as he fell to his knees)
the branches a friendly smile.

Raindrops on the tree made the tree so
beautiful to him, for this one willow tree
seemed to sparkle like no other tree could
be, within a special moment he knew he was
not alone, that no one could take the part of
this friendship a willow tree could bring,
he had found a friend.

With raindrops in his hair, he stood up
strong and looked up at his tree, he gave
a friendly smile and reaching out his
hand he took his friend and walked
away.

Fun to Be

This is completely different,
just for something new,
I thought I'd send this
with thoughts to you.

Have a lovely day, and enjoy
your way, as you go on with
your day, and have fun along
the way.

Dedication

To all the pets I knew,
my thoughts are always
with you, for the friendship
that was there I was never
in despair.

Thank you for all the times,
being there at all times,
words can not express
how much I want to say,
I wish you were here today,
for it is not fair you went
away.

The few of you I knew, I was
never blue, how I miss you too,
this is dedicated with love to you.

The Open Door

The empty feeling left inside,
no one can imagine what a feeling
that can hide.

The empty feeling behind the door
that seems to close more and more,
with each push you try and try, but
all you do is cry and cry, you lie in
wait for that magic moment that one
day the door will open, the day may
one day come the struggle to be no more,
and there lies the beauty of the future
to bring once in a forgotten world lost
long ago.

That magic moment when you reach
outside the door, you walk through
and see a world that you once never
knew, it's up to you to see this through,
for only you can remember the world
you once knew.

Future to Be

It's really hard when everyday is
the same, sometimes I think it's all
a game, is it a test, or is it not, how
long must we wait and see for a
world to be kind to me.

To be happy as it can ever be.
To see a future that was once
was, to be free to be me.

Walking to the Future

Let me take you by the hand and walk with you,
we shall walk and talk as far away as you want
to, with each step we take we find two paths,
one will lead us very far and long, the other
will keep us very near.

The long journey will be journey not revealed,
the short journey stands as we see it now,
we stand and wonder which paths to take,
it is a decision we all must take,
let it never be too late, which decision would
you make?

Take a longer walk and see for now or near
thus not you fear,
though not known what is far away,
take a closer look and see, for if you
go through this long road there may be
a lot to learn,
if you stay at the short road you will never
know and never see what the future will bring
afar you see,
so thank you for taking this walk with me,
for now you see a future that will be.

Deep Words

Treasure all that is, for life
is precious and words can
never be found to say how
important it is to be around.

Think of something you
like to do, and fulfill that
if you will.

Hope

Have faith in yourself,
walk each day one step
at a time remembering
you are only human and
much loved, never be too
hard on yourself, keep on
this wonderful journey you
are heading for.

The big picture is clear now
you have come as far as you
have.

Life is an amazing journey,
if people let you down, hold
your head high and
remembering you will never
be alone,
there will be someone there to
take this journey with you.

Expressions

It has always got me through
rain or shine, and from time to
time I would draw to pass the
time, we all are special with a
talent to give, find yours, for
please do see it. Sometimes you may
have to go through something
to see the real you, to see the
talent that you had never known,
but when you find what you are
looking for, you will see but
through that door a talent
waiting for you, that has been
there all along, so reach out for
that special gift, for you are
special and have a lot to give.

To Fly Away

If you were a bird would you fly away?
Would you fly to a tree, or would you sit
by me? If you did fly high, what would
you see? Would you see the world like
me?

What would you think if you had a thought,
would you run and hide, or would you stand
by me?

What a wonderful world it would be to fly
high, to see the world as you see.

A Reflection on One Self

To those who missed a childhood,
one they never knew. It is sad to see
the ones who have been left behind.

The ones who find it hard to find what they
never know. Do not worry, my friend, for you
will find not too far away what you are looking for.
Accept what once has happened and look out for today.

With these words I say so you can. You cannot change
what was yesterday, but please don't despair. The future is
today, so therefore hold no fear.

Bonded

We walk together, my friend
and I, we stay close by, and share
many a thought, he speaks to me
my friend he does, his words so
precious, his meaning so true, I
could never be blue, for the bond
so strong, he stays with me beside
my side through thick and thin,
through rain and shine.

It matters to him in many ways,
to be with me till the end of days
and there beside me he stays.

Inspired

If you are in a garden and sat and
watched the sky, what colour would
it be? What would you see?
As you watched the flowers all a
different colour, would you smile
and sit there for a while?
As you sat watching for a
moment always consider
the beauty that surrounds you that's
always been around.

We sometimes forget what is there
for us to see, for there is beauty
every where you see.

The Sand Through Our Eyes

At the thought of the moment, I walk through the sand,
the soft warm feeling left behind me as I stand,
a look in the distance, I feel the sand
and watch it slowly go through my hand.

The clear white snow all around me I know, before me, beyond me, and across the way, this beautiful white sand a reach not far away.

I stand and walk with sand in my hand, I reach for the sky throwing the sand to the air, slowly watching, sea in the background, the sand to the shore, what a wonderful feeling that's in store, for this sand that's here is beautiful to see and a beautiful feeling for me.

Lost and Gone

Does it matter, or does it not, the
the kindness that have been put out,
have I not always been there, have I
not, thus so easy to forget the things
that I have done for you.

To be insensitive is to be strong, but
I must say I forgot the more sensitive
that I am, the more hurt I got.

Where are you my friend? Have you
forgotten me have you not?

It is up to you if you stay or not,
but I have given you a lot, please
do not forget me as I say, that not
everybody goes away, as you can
see I am still your friend today, for
I am happy this way.

Please understand it will be just fine
to reach out, why give up on me my
friend, my feelings torn at every end,
as you can see deep down inside, I have
never given up on you and pushed you
aside, so hear my plea my good friend
please come sit beside and be my friend.

The Friend in You

Always, believe in one self, care for
those around you, be a part of the world
that surrounds you, reach out high and tall,
but do not be afraid to fall, it is fine to make
mistakes.

I know it is hard to climb that wall, but make
that first step, it is there always waiting for you,
so go on then, make it happen, for it is fine to be
afraid, what is behind there, but you will never
know if you don't have a go.

It will take time I know, but you will know when
to take that step, it's all in a meaning that we do
not understand, but above that wall you will see,
so hold your head and be strong, climb that wall
for on the other side of the wall, there is a friend
to catch your fall.

Friends

To everyone I know, these
words are dedicated to you,
for being there, for being fair,
for seeing things through, for
your courage.

I thank you for your kindness
and your thoughts, not being
afraid to share, to reach out,
for not going away,
for without you it would not
been fun.

So thank you to you my special
friends, those that will be with
me to the end.

The Waterfall

Sitting beside you I am inspired, holding
you in my hand I feel the cool on my face,
which gives me a warm embrace.

I splash you on my hair, drops slowly
dripping down on the rocks where I sit,
you sit there with me, I hear the flow of
you gently running down stream to water
below, oh how you glow, the air so crisp.

I look up at the sky, I watch the clouds go
by, I give a sigh, and I never want to say
goodbye, for you are so beautiful.

I hear the birds a many song, the flowers
all a splendid colour.

The leaves on the ground I run in my hand,
I put them in the water, and watch them fly.

The joy, I hold on this day, how wonderful
it is to enjoy what I see, it's clear to me that
what I see is magical, for us all to see, this
waterfall sitting here beside me, makes me
feel so good you see.

I lay down and hear you, as I close my eyes,
I never want to leave your side.

The warmth you give me in my heart, the flow I hear is very dear, so my waterfall thank you for my inspiration today I hold you very near.

Brothers and Sisters

A wish for this, sharing thoughts with,
shopping with, going to school with, I
never had this, growing up without you,
I did miss this, not having you to talk
with, I did wish for this.

Having thought all about this, I reflect
back on what is missed and I only now
wish for a brother and sister to be here
that I can hold very dear.

Our World

It's so much a rush, why is it so?
Everybody must be in a hurry,
everybody race round and round
running themselves to the ground,
it seems you are always running,
but all you're doing is going in a
big circle, for what you do to make
that pay, it's not easy I say, how the
world has to be this way.

Take it easy and relax, it's fine if you
do that you see, do not be too busy to do
something for yourself, for you are
special as life itself.

To Remember

Waiting for that call, the one that
does not ring, why is it so, why
must it be so hard, please do not
say you will ring, and then do not.

Why is it important that call to be?
Why must we wait to see if that call
will ever come to thee.

Closely Near

To all that I hold close and very near,
thank you so much for standing so near,
for holding me high, for sticking by and
not saying goodbye.

Through the rough times and happy times,
I dedicate this verse with love to you.

Friendship is strong, I know I am not wrong,
and we have been through a lot, that I have
not forgot.

The many years have passed and we have
seen through it all, it has been fun and I have
enjoyed the lot, and I owe it all to you.

Thank you for your patience, together we
stand, hand in hand, together we walk and
talk.

We share your thoughts so closely near,
my friend that's dear.

Shining Star

If you climb a big long wall,
just be careful you do not fall,
just be brave and stand up tall,
break down those barriers, that
way they will become very small,
do not cry, be proud of who you
are, you have come very far.

Look up at a shining star, for it's
not as far, hold it within your heart
and let it be just the start of something
big and something bright, go fly away
and let the magic of the star capture the
light within that lovely moment.

There is always hope, so do not worry,
and never leave in a hurry, that shining
star, the one that you're holding that is not
afar.

Take it with you as you walk through that
wall, that was so lonely, stand brave,
remember that shining star, that has helped
you through those gates.

Because of You

If it was not for you, I would not
have met you, if it was not for you,
I would not have changed my
direction, if it was not for you, I
would not be inspired, if it was not
for you, I would have known one less,
if it was not for you, I would be blue,
that's true, for everyone I thank you
for being you.

If it was not for you, there would be no
connection with who I know today, and
I owe it all to you.

Thank you for connecting me with those
I know today, this is true, because of you
I am now not blue, thank you.

A Pet's Friend

Mimi is my little friend, someone
that I will have to the end.

We stay together just the two of us,
never has there been a fuss, her little
chatter means a lot, for my little friend
is quite the boss.

I love my little Mimi, for without her
It would be a lose, so here we go hand
in hand, my little Mimi and I.

Hope we never have to say goodbye.

Clouds of Wonder

A many different look, so fascinating you are, beautiful white, with so many shapes and sizes.

The story you do tell, you seem to move with ease gliding into the breeze.

The birds flying under you, raindrops coming from you, planes flying over you.

I have to wonder how you sparkle in the sky as you glide by, you look so beautiful, you do, I wish I can hold you in my hand, when you disappear in the breeze I want to take a photo.

This wonder of a cloud, brings joy and fascination, how lovely you do look, I just had to add you to my book.

Never Easy

For you, for I have not forgotten,
the gifts you gave, for taking care
to be there for a person who needed
you to care, you stayed with and I
know you have done your best.

You never gave up
it takes a special person to see things
through, for I can see this in you,
thankyou.

Mum

You did your best therefore I am grateful, it is so hard to see you this way, there is no answer I can give why life has turned this way for you, but there is a reason I am sure, I come to see you, I always ring you, I send you photos, I love you dearly, could have tried a lot more, but all I did was cry a lot more.

Thank you so much for what you have done, for without you I would have none.

Not to be Forgotten

Please do not forget me, I am very dear,
do my best at times, that's clear, deep down
I know I am not forgotten, but it is hard to
see this when you're in the moment.

Thank you for what I do have, for our nature
our animals, our friends and family, may we
not forget what we do have, thank you.

I will continue to enjoy what is around me,
for my talents I will not forget, those close
to me I thank you for, those afar, I thank you
for, I will not forget you, for you are very dear.

I know you have not forgotten me, my friend,
and that you are very near.

Always a Person

It does not matter what job you do.
Whether you work in a zoo, or polish
a shoe, there is always something to
do that will be important to you.

To be happy in what you do will
mean a lot to you, and you know
that's the job for you.

Take care in what you do, make it
fun and worthwhile, to be that
person if you will, to work hard
and be proud of what you do,
never be afraid to see it through,
therefore you can see the person
in you that's true, and the real you.

Nature

The many different colours,
so beautiful you are, you sway
in the breeze, your leaves fall
a many shade.

The sun shines on you, that's true
the rain drops capture your delightful
colours a picture in the breeze.

The colours that surround me, I sit
with you with ease, feeling so free,
I can now see what you mean to me.

I capture the moment as you sit there
beside me, I look up at the sky, I see
what surrounds and I smile, what a
moment to capture, what a delight to
see, how precious you are
to see.

My Journey so Far

This is my journey so far, a lot to learn and a lot to see, for it has not been easy for me, but I do see how it can be, for now I am clear, and I see no fear.

I look around and see what life is all about.

To those who took this journey with me, I may not know you, but I understand what you have been through, remember it is fine, but please remember don't stay this way, find a way to reach out, and you will find your way.

We all have to go through things, be easy be it not, you are not forgot.

To Belong

Hold your head not to the floor, thus hold up high and strong, just like you belong.

   To all that gave me strength

   To those who stood by my

   Dedicated to all I know

      with love.

www.ingramcontent.com/pod-product-compliance
Lightning Source LLC
Chambersburg PA
CBHW071039080526
44587CB00015B/2685